ODD FELLOWS

PETE MARSHALL

CinnamonPress

INDEPENDENT INNOVATIVE INTERNATIONAL

Published by Cinnamon Press
Meirion House
Tanygrisiau
Blaenau Ffestiniog
Gwynedd, LL41 3SU
www.cinnamonpress.com

British Library Cataloguing in Publication Data. A CIP record for this book can be obtained from the British Library.

Designed and typeset in Palatino by Cinnamon Press. Printed in Poland.

Cover design by Adam Craig.

Cinnamon Press is represented in the UK by Inpress Ltd and in Wales by the Welsh Books Council.

Acknowledgements

Poems from this book originally appeared in the following literary magazines:-
Orbis, Envoi, Bog, Folded Sheets, Flash, Poetry Wales and *Tears In The Fence.*

'A good day to die,' first appeared in *Past Tense,* a Liquorice Fish Anthology.

'Tazzer,' 'Gwenno,' and 'Cwm,' first appeared in *Agog,* a collection of poetry and prose, published by Cinnamon Press.

'Teds, circa 1974/76,' first appeared in *What Lies Within,* a liquorice Fish Anthology.

Thanks again to Jan and Adam at the amazing Cinnamon Press for their on-going faith, friendship, advice and support.

Contents

Many thanks are due to Mr. Nick Pilgrim (aka: Big Nose), entrepreneur and patron of the arts, for his kind and generous support of this work.

Odd Fellows

To Jacquie, the one and only love of my life.
Oh, and to Deri, Joe and Nansi, my fantastic kids,
who I love also. In a different way. Obviously.

And to the Odd Fellows.
Who don't know who they are.

soup

She was always there when he came home from school.

The small kitchen smelled of tomato soup.

Heinz Tomato Soup.

The spoon was always on the table next to the bowl and three pieces of Mother's Pride bread would have been cut into squares and placed on a small plate next to the bowl. Always twelve squares of soft white bread.

The strange thing was that she always put a fork on the table too. Next to the bowl and the spoon and the twelve square pieces of soft white Mother's Pride bread.

He would take off his blazer, hang it on the back of the wooden chair, then pull out the chair, carefully, trying not to make it scrape across the floor, trying to make sure it didn't make any noise.

Then he would sit down and wait for her to pour the soup into the bowl.

This happened every day.

And every day he would dip four pieces of bread into the soup and eat them. And then he would pick up the spoon and eat some of the soup. Then he would put the spoon down and dip four pieces of bread into the soup and eat them. Then he would pick up the spoon and eat some of the soup. Finally he would put the spoon down and dip the last four pieces of bread and eat them before picking up the spoon again and eating the soup with it until the soup was finished.

Then the soup would be gone and she would take the bowl and the spoon and the plate and the fork and put them in the sink.

And now, fifty years later, sitting at a different table, he still remembers the fork...not the soup, or the bread, or the woman, or the taste, or the smell...the fork.

Why the fork?

Always the fork.

Teds, circa 1974/76

…we were cut throated visionaries

hard as cotton candy

innocent as fish hooks

authentic as teeth pulled from a plastic comb

lip curlers in brothel creepers and boot lace ties who sulked for the cameras and rode bench seat Galaxy caravans on frenzied migrations to half suspecting coastal towns

    where

preening velvet plumage we'd roost in bars brooding with adolescent nonchalance over the pony tailed and stilettoed girls who flocked along the prom while on the pier speakers blasted rock 'n' roll twenty years too late for all except the draped and winkle picking originals who bopped and jived with pot-bellied sincerity their mock-brylcreem quiffs salt lacquered by the breeze...

from the mouths of babes

1

*in the High Court the defendant argued that no plagiarism had taken place indeed
stated loudly that he had not stolen any of the poems, he had found them:*

Poetry is three mismatched shoes at the entrance of a dark alley;
is a sofa full of blind singers who have put aside their canes,
it is speech in which the words come in an order which could not
be changed without ruining the verity and power of the whole;

poetry's a zoo in which you keep demons and angels, deep gossip,
it is a dame with a huge pedigree, philosophy's sister (the one who
wears the make-up). It is a kind of leaving notes for someone else
to find, and a willingness for them to fall into the wrong hands.

Poetry is the rapture of rhythmical language, it makes the invisible
appear, it is a way of talking about things that frighten you;
poetry is a machine for remembering itself, it is a way of communi-
cating a vast array of thoughts and feelings, it is a trick, and a

poem is an attempt to find the music in the words describing an
intuition, a smuggling of something back from the otherworld,
a prime bit of shoplifting, a ghost seeking substantiality. A poem
has to be the most powerful thing one can say in the shortest space

possible.

2

*informed their worships that if a crime had indeed been committed he eagerly
awaited the court's sentence as it would finally reveal to him poetry's true value:*

As with any other product there is no justice in the marketing
and consumption of poetry. Just as the richest people are prone
to regard capitalism as even-handed, so the most successful
poets are the likeliest to assume the business is a pure meritocracy;

a poetry bestseller is one that sells four or five copies in any store,
poets are the *Big Issue* sellers of the literary world, some are silent
and desperate, others mad and messianic, you know you ought to
buy their wares but suspect you won't enjoy them...

Poets and money are seen in each other's company only rarely, they
can do without money—a good thing, as they have more aesthetic
freedom precisely because nobody cares how or what they write;
poems are chits that get you off work. To devote a life

to poetry looks like a decision to ignore the benefits of modern
living, it looks a lot like sulking. The impulse to write poetry is the
enemy because it's keeping you poor. The hope of permanent fame
may be the second silliest motive for writing poetry, the first is—

the hope for untold riches.

3

harangued in the stocks the poet publicly apologised to the poets from whom the poetry had been pilfered:

A special gift isn't bestowed on us by God but by another god—
Hard Work. I was my own creator. All people talk to themselves,
some are overheard—they are the poets. To be a published poet is
not a sane aspiration, any fool can write poetry but it takes a genius

to get it published; if you are writing poetry only to get published
you belong in some other kind of writing. And, what's more, if
artistic work is done without the artist committing his whole
self the effect is dubious; poetry should be old as time, poets used

to be mad or bad now they are mostly just sad. There are *jealousies*
rolling about—not much chinking money—plenty of *grinding teeth.*
The one thing gets a poet irritated is the thought of another poet's
poems. Heavyweight boxing is tame compared with the contests

of literary men. It is surprising how much grousing goes on
in the name of poetry. It is tribal. The sense of ferrets fighting for
mastery of the sceptic tank is depressing, the tension Oedipal.
There's nothing like a punch in the mouth to remind you

your poem wasn't as clever as you thought.

up yours I'm a poet

…you're 'avin' a larf incha
i'd sooner put pins in me eyes
            than read that shite
which don't even fuckin' rhyme
            and evocative
wots all that about then
            evocative my arse

and Pentre Ifan burial chamber

if that's not just a fuckin' pile of
            old stones
you can kiss my fat hairy
            ring piece…

            Newgale:
England beat the French
as the brainsbellied locals
            jeered them on;
we stayed and drank, and drank,
            and drank, until
the salty girls were gone

then onto the beach at midnight;
pebblefooted, stumbledrunk,
futon mattress in the surf,
draining the Paddy,
searching for the key to
Druidstone's Haven,
            singing songs,
weeping loud and lairy wideboy tears
mourning the passage
            of the years

    ...so there's ol' Bassy
all Essex boy and pikey
off on a Welsh jolly wiv his mucker
'e's there in the mornin'
all whiskey breaf and cider sweat
'e's chucked open the flap
stuck his boat race out the tent
and 'e can't Adam and Eve it
straight-up-on-my-life
as I live and breave
'e's only gone and woken up
                    in a fuckin' poem...

Theodore's Penitential and the Witch

in the old church the young Welsh priest with the mad ram's wool hair and crazy black eyes raises his pale hands to the ancient oak rafters and glaring at the subdued and subservient congregation bans:

Idolatry and the worship of demons
The cult of the dead
Worship of nature (trees, wells, stones etc.)
Pagan calendar customs and festivals
Witchcraft and sorcery (necromancy)
Surgery and divination
Astrology

meanwhile, outside, in the Llan, the Welsh witch with the Celtic red hair and green eyes and Yew staff takes the skin-sickly child by the hand, leads it to the to the well and lays the child on the stone, removes the child's sack cloth garments and dips them into the spring, wrings them dry and places them back upon the child whose skin disease is cured

and the Welsh priest wails

'no one shall go to the trees, or wells, or stones, or enclosures (circles) or anywhere else but to God's holy church'

meanwhile, outside in the Llan, the Welsh witch carries the crippled child to the well and lays the child on the stone, she takes the pin from the child's cloak, bends it and drops it into the spring then retrieves the pin, straightens it and plunges it into the crippled child's thighs and the child is cured and walks away

and the Welsh priest cries

'let no Christian place lights at the temples, or at the stones, or at the fountains, or at trees, or enclosures, or at places where three ways meet'

meanwhile, outside in the Llan, the Welsh witch guides the blind child to the well and lays the child on the stone, she dips an adder's skin into the spring and then places the skin on the child's eyes and the child is cured and can see

and the Welsh priest shrieks

'let no one presume to make lustrations, or to enchant herbs, or to make flocks pass through a hollow tree or an aperture in the earth for by doing so they seem to consecrate themselves to the devil'

meanwhile, outside in the Llan, the Welsh witch guides the dumb child to the well and lays the child on the stone and places the child's belt in the spring and then wraps the belt around the child's throat and the child is cured and can speak and the child says 'praise the Lord'

Polruan

for Caz

first thing

in the lane behind the house
slippered biddies cackle and yawl

later

on the flagged patio
a suntrapped brandy hangover

ginger cat in a ginger dinghy

Comanche gulls wheeling in a clotted bluesky;

a school bell rings

(memories of playground laughter
of shrill boys and giddy girls)

further out mowermoan and strimmerclatter
an outboard gurgles in the bay

and next door, on a whitewashed scaffold,
old Zennor drawls Cornish into an iphone;

noonish

a ziggerzagger slate-stepped stroll to the harbour

where hi-viz trawlermen, wellied and braced,
flirt with lycra'd grockles

and the laughing ferryman calls
—*come on now my lovelies*—

and at The Lugger
whitebait and bubbled jugs of Rattler

the old boy on the bench
with the pipe and the pint and the pasty
and the weatherworn face

smiles and nods and winks and says

proper job

the terminal ceiling

His plane was delayed as usual and I swore that this time, if he arrived pissed, I'd just walk away and leave him to look after himself.

I killed an hour in the concourse drinking coffee. Then another hour going up and down the walkways, trying to get the girls who passed slowly by on the other side to smile. Sometimes they did, sometimes they didn't, but mostly they did and it made me happy to think that I could still make a pretty girl smile, even at my age.

I made my way back to the arrivals' gate.

They were last out.

He had his arm around her. She was beautiful. His new bright and shiny all paid for stunningly beautiful Thai bride.

He saw me and smiled and raised his hand. I waved back. He walked forward with his arms outstretched and held me in an embrace. I had a fleeting memory of our childhood together and how much we had fought and how much we had loved each other.

I could see her over his shoulder looking unsure, looking shy and confused; I gave her a wink and she looked at her feet.

Then somebody behind her shouted something. There was a brief brilliant flash of light and I felt my brother throwing me backwards, upwards, away from him, up into the air, up towards the terminal ceiling.

In slow motion.

As if I were light as feather. Or a balloon filled with gas. Or a bubble from an aqualung slowly rising to the surface of the sea. Or a meadowlark soaring a cappella into a clear blue summer sky.

I was on the terminal ceiling. Or, more precisely, hovering a few inches beneath the terminal ceiling. The light was so bright that I couldn't see anything. But I couldn't close my eyes and I couldn't shield my eyes from the light.

My arms were by my side.

I couldn't move my arms.

But I could hear a noise. A white noise. The noise of water. Not water running. Not a river. A swimming pool; the hollow echo of water in a swimming pool. And I could hear a dull drone as if there were a pump, behind me, in the roof. Or a generator working in the walls.

I stayed still for a long time.

Something was holding me up. Some kind of force. Some kind of gravitational or magnetic force.

After a while some feeling came back into my hands and I found that if I fanned them gently, the way you would if you were floating on your back in a swimming pool, using my hands like fins, like the tiny fins of an angel fish, I could rotate slowly. Rotate slowly on the terminal ceiling. I couldn't move forward or backward or sideways. I could just rotate slowly, clockwise, on the terminal ceiling.

Like an angel fish.

Like I used to when I was a child, off school, ill.

A fevered child off school ill in bed watching the cracks in the walls expand and contract. Rotating slowly on his sick bed in a fevered delirium.

Then, after a very long time, there was another noise.

A noise that I didn't like.

A whirring sound. Like a fan in a wind turbine. Like a fan drawing smoke out of a tunnel. A fan sucking the brilliant light out of the terminal, draining away whatever force had been keeping me on the terminal ceiling.

And then I heard the screaming.

As I fell.

Or was pulled.

Down.

And as I fell I saw the chaos below me. Saw the people running in panic. Saw the carnage and the rivers of blood and the gore and the bits of people scattered around the concourse.

But I couldn't see my brother.

Or his stunningly beautiful Thai bride.

Then somebody was holding my hand and telling me that I was going to be OK. But I wasn't OK. And I knew I was never going to be OK again. I just wanted to get back on the terminal ceiling.

I remember wishing that I could be back on the terminal ceiling.

O.P.

The O.P. was the last terraced house in a row of Catholic houses that had been burned out by the Prots at the start of the troubles. It had an observation post upstairs with a grill that looked out onto the patch. It had a bedroom with four bunk beds and downstairs it had a kitchen and sitting room. The houses next to it had been bricked in so the Provo's couldn't bomb the place. Outside it was surrounded by steel mesh to keep off the R.P.G.s and petrol bombs. The brick got dropped off by Pig and the previous occupants got picked up. Their job was to keep watch over the patch. Monitor the comings and goings of the I.R.A. into and out of the area. And set up road blocks if there was an incident. They weren't supposed to leave the O.P. but occasionally they liked to sneak out and hide so that when the local lads turned up to stone and lob Molotov's at the wire, usually on a Friday or Saturday night after the drinking clubs shut down, they could jump out with their batons and give them a good hiding. It was a well-liked job. Easy and not too dangerous. Good food and decent sleeping arrangements. One of the bricks, under the command of Bombardier Campbell also had the benefit of some female company. They'd met and got friendly with a couple of girls during a foot patrol and Gunner Rowe, a good looking Devon lad, had suggested they meet up at the O.P. next time they were on duty. Sure enough the girls, Rena and Colleen, turned up and hung around outside the wire one afternoon and got let into the O.P. This became a regular thing. Every time Campbell and Rowe and the lads were at the O.P. the girls would turn up and get let in. The girls would bring booze with them and a good time was had by all. The boys were all decent lads. So there was no funny business. Well not much funny business. They'd play strip poker a lot. The boys would end up in their skiddies. And the girls would end up half naked, dressed up in the boys' uniforms, saluting and doing drill with the lads' rifles. Having a laugh. Gunner Ginge Burns took photos of them all together arm in arm and then, not being the brightest of lads, when they got back to camp he gave the film to an R.U.C. police sergeant to get it developed. Of course the Prot in the shop who developed the pics told the R.U.C. man who looked at them and told the M.P.s who looked at them and told the Regimental Lt Colonel who busted Campbell down to gunner and who said that he would punish them all properly when they got back to Germany because he couldn't afford to jail them on active service because he needed boots on the ground. The R.U.C. man told other people. When they found Rena and Colleen they had been tied to a lamp post, heads shaved, tarred and feathered and knee-capped.

the power of prayer

our father who art in heaven
(my Aunt Fanny)

listen, I hate to be the bearer of bad tidings,
but on the divine intervention front
the Messiah really sucked

a sliding scale of desperation

pleaseGodpleaseLordpleaseJesusplease
make it go away
make him better
guide the surgeon's hand
make the therapy work
get him on the trial
give him more time
make it quick
end it now

panic prayers flung into the void

and there was nothing

    zip
    nada

    no,
    not nothing,

nothing might have been bearable

instead he chose to tease and toy
to give false hope
then snatch it away
like a capricious lover
or a vicious kid

so

one day, Jesus old lad, we're going to have words
        you and me
there are going to be questions asked
and if you don't come up
with some pretty good answers
I'm going to take that shiny halo of yours
and shove it right up your holy arse

Simple Simon's Meet

Opposite, grotesque drift-goblin leer; chill
barrow-breath howls spawning snow devils
that dance and spiral on hard pack ice
before him. Raised up from the bright road
a discordant cacophony; spectrally the myriad
shrill voices call his most secret names.

Witness, through fur-lined tunnel vision,
ephemeral flakes silently filling footprints.
It's too cold for him. Involuntary spliced
video images of the morning's strangulations
flood his twisting mind; Hitchcock's man,
in shadow, knotted scarf raised.

Pressing against blue denim zipper prison
the erection is painful; yellow silk
throttle stocking bites deep into finger.
Then yet again the phantom choir calls;
Soon Simple Simon, she'll be here soon.
He levels his arm. Thumb raised.

Sonnet for Tracey

Shall I compare thee to a lovely fish?
I meant a dolphin not a bleedin' trout!
I'm trying to say that you're a pukka dish,
Oh come on Tracey sweetheart leave it out.
Right, up yours, I'm going down the pub
For pints and porky scratchings with me mates.
You never got it did you? There's the rub,
You never understood me poet's traits.
Now, just let me say it one more time in rhyme,
I love you, like a cod loves parsley sauce,
So come on gorgeous while I'm in me prime
Jump on me Trace and ride me like a horse:
    For you to me are everything
    The sweetest song that I can sing
        (oh baby!)

the poet and the muse
and the wife and the husband

This sort of thing has to be a chance encounter, a fluke.

It has to be unplanned.

You cannot meet a muse on a dating site.

In this case then, the poet lives on a farm in Wales and, realising that he cannot make any money out of being a poet, has converted barns into holiday cottages. The muse lives on a ranch in Colorado, her husband has a business trip planned in London and they intend to visit Wales afterwards. The muse contacts the poet to see if she can rent a cottage from him. He is fully booked. The muse books a cottage in the next village.

The muse is 40 something and happily married with 3 kids. She loves her husband and kids very much. But she is half Shoshone Indian and she has inherited her ancestors' wild nature and her tribe's wanderlust. She is very beautiful with dark skin, brown eyes and long black hair.

The poet is 50 something and happily married with 3 kids. He loves his wife and kids very much. But his ancestors were Romany Tinkers and he has inherited their wild nature and peoples' wanderlust. He is very handsome with dark skin, brown eyes and long black hair.

The muse's husband is a rancher and banker. He is a good man. He is a solid, dependable, hardworking and moral man who loves his wife unreservedly. He doesn't understand the muse's wild side.

The wife is long suffering. She has had to put up with the poet's crazy antics for 25 plus years. But she loves him. And, being an artist herself, knows that to be a real poet you have to be a little wild and a little insane. She has cut the poet a lot of slack.

After the first contact the poet and the muse stay in touch. They email each other a lot. She loves Europe. He loves America. Within weeks they feel as if they have known each other all their lives. They talk about love and life and faith and their experiences so far and their hopes and dreams and they tell each other things that they have never told anybody else.

And then, inexplicably, and not by design, at exactly the same moment they press send and email each other photos of themselves.

And, of course, it cannot be any other way, when the photographs appear on the screens in front of them, simultaneously, they stare into each other's eyes and topple headlong over the top and into the brink.

The poet and the muse plan to meet when the muse and her family come to the cottage in the next village. They talk about how great it will be to meet each other's partners and children. But in their hearts they know this is an act of desperation and at the last moment, realising that it would be folly, that they wouldn't be able to hide their true feelings for each other and that they would cause hurt and embarrassment to their families, to the people they love, they call it off.

And, sadly, with great personal hurt and emotion, they agree to do the right thing and end what they both now realise is a love and a passion that is ultimately and inevitably doomed.

But, of course, as is the nature of these things, we know they can't.

It is already too late.

So when the muse and her family arrive at the hillside cottage the poet emails her and begs and pleads for her to meet him. And of course the muse says no. And the poet, using all his skill, continues to beg and tells her he will die if he doesn't meet her, even if it is only for the briefest of moments. Even if it is only once. And, in the end, blinded by love and desire, she agrees and she slips out of the cottage at midnight when her family are fast asleep and walks slowly and gently down through the rolling meadows and misty pastures to meet the poet who is waiting for her by the beach.

Without hesitation they rush into each other's arms and embrace and when they kiss for the first time a jolt of kinetic energy passes between them and they feel weak and helpless and overawed by the power that now binds them together. And they walk hand in hand along the strand, not speaking, listening to the sounds of the estuary, breathless and aware only of the waves of love passing between them like the tide crashing onto the beach.

They walk slowly to the little town and they walk slowly arm in arm around the town walls and they climb over the gate into the castle and up the spiral staircase to The Lovers' Tower and lying together on the cold leaded cupola they gaze into a sky awash with a myriad glistening stars and a pale yellow moon hangs heavy over the mountains and when they make love it is the most intensely erotic and passionate experience of their lives and they are reduced to tears at the thought that they will soon have to part.

On the walk back they tell each other that this love they have found is crazy and foolish and they must leave it behind for their sake, and for the sakes of all the people they care for. But when they leave each other, and the muse walks up through the pasture and the meadow to her family, and the poet returns to his, the depth of their grief and overwhelming sense of pain is so great that they are both already bereft and in mourning.

But, of course, as is the nature of these things, we know they cannot let it go.

It is already too late.

Needless to say the end game is fairly swift and predictable.

The poet tells the wife about the affair and tells her he cannot live without the muse. The wife tells him he is a fool, she tells him he has a wife and a family and that it is them who he should love. The poet tells her he has to go to her. The wife tells him that if he does she will never have him back. Enough is enough she tells him.

The poet tells the muse he is coming.

The muse tells him it is mad and he shouldn't.

The poet flies to Denver and emails the muse and begs her to meet him and she cannot refuse him and they meet and feel the same as they had in Wales and swear undying and eternal love to each other and without telling the husband the muse elopes on a crazy road trip of the American West with the poet and they drink cold beer and bourbon in bars in Cheyenne and Laramie and Jackson and Cody and Deadwood like a latter day Bonny and Clyde and using her as inspiration the poet writes decadent love poems and the muse dances for the poet in her moccasins and a deer skin dress embroidered with beads and porcupine-quills and they make love on the high plains and in the mountains and on the prairie and in the desert.

They are finally overtaken on the outskirts of Tombstone, Arizona, by a contemporary posse made up of the husband and his four brothers, all cowboys and ranchers, who drag the poet from the car and proceed to beat him to within an inch of his life while the muse screams and cries and begs for mercy, begs for them to stop, and her anguish and tears drives them into an even wilder frenzy and they leave the poet in the desert for dead.

The muse is taken back to Colorado by the posse, and the husband, who has virtually lost his sanity because of the betrayal and grief, keeps her locked away in the ranch house like a virtual prisoner.

The poet is found by a Chiricahua Apache and taken to hospital. He spends many many months in America in intensive care before being flown home by air ambulance. The wife has to sell the farm to pay for his medical bills. She refuses to speak to him again. The wife spends the rest of her life in poverty.

The poet has irreparable spinal injuries and is told he will spend the rest of his life in a wheel chair. The muse does not answer any of his emails or letters or calls. He cannot write. He takes to drink. Less than a year later later he pushes his wheel chair into the sea at the beach where he first met her.

The muse manages to sneak a letter out to the poet. It goes to the farm and the new owner re-directs it to the wife who feels she has the moral duty to write back to the muse telling her about the poet's death.

The muse escapes and flies to the U.K. She makes her way to the little town, walks the walls, climbs the spiral staircase to the top of the Lovers' Tower and jumps.

When the husband hears the news of her death he saddles his favourite Palomino mare, rides out into the Rockies, and blows his brains out with an antique pearl handled Colt Peacemaker.

See. Same old same old.

Suicidal Jez down The Odds 1983

Over at the Motorola Video Juke Box
a bad case of robotoid histrionics;

slender piano-forte fingers punching
bland designer selections at random.

He whirls, manic, zig-zags to feed
pockets full of shrapnel into a gutsy
fruitless machine void.

Spins again.

Surveys the scene with a baleful eye
(speeding strobe monster stalks prey)

spots me
        damn it
                lurches over

to sit and smile and smile and smile and
in a catechism of funk and fluorescence
shoot high velocity nonsense from the lip.

so now her nets are cast

slight simian grey antiquity
shuffles withered in worn
Turkish slippered exhibition
a feeble non-artefact of an older
dust free heritage;

she awaits we think a pinch
or preview of her dinners
current motivation for she
hungers still behind her
thinning cut glass auditorium;

and waiting merely twenty four
hours a minute for this month's
Young Socialist Worker's weekly
visiting time she clocks the
sundial by the milkman's float;

so now her nets are cast onto
thumb tacks or arrow slits
or hanging baskets full of
sorry echoes whispered by all
but none but her

invocations

once

on a flat ledge
overlooking a gorge
in Crete
I conjured Pan

a cloven clatter

an overwhelming stench
of rot and rut

the rising hairlipped wail
of a goat god

which had me running

for the comfort
of retsina and ouzo

(when you died)

the lights went out
on the Migneint

trees grew quiet in Coed Mawr

wells ran dry in churches

twins felt no pain

and the stones
ceased their humming

but last night

the white owl
on the big barn
turned his moonface
full circle

      and winked

Big Nose and Ix

Things changed dramatically for The DripTrays when Big Nose and Ix bought the house in Lionfield Terrace, just off Arbour Lane, just down the road from the Odds. This was back in the day when pubs called last orders at 10:30 and closed at 11. Even Fatty Belly and Oddy only had sessions on the occasional Thursday, Friday and Saturday nights. So usually the boys had to secrete cans of Party Seven or cartons of rank wine or bottles of cheap cider in hidey places and glug them in bus shelters or public toilets or down the Bunny Walks. Number 9, Lionfield Terrace was open all the time and there was always a dedicated crew of DripTrays imbibing there. Anytime. Day or night. There were no rules. At all. I myself lived for 6 weeks on a bed of high quality Scandinavian porn in a louvered wardrobe in Ix's room. Ix was a loud and vigorous lover who sounded a bit like the Flying Scotsman when he was at it, so often I found it hard to nod off. Many a time I had to apologise to one of his naked lovers when I burst out of the wardrobe, interrupting their passion, because I needed a vindaloo dump or a Bob and Abbot slash. Two films, Apocalypse Now and The Blues Brothers, were on a constant loop. People crashed everywhere (on the floor, in any bed left vacant, in toilets, leaning against walls, in the attic, in any car left unlocked, in the garden, in the garden shed, in the neighbours garden shed,) some of them unknown to Big Nose or Ix or anybody else. And there were often girls there. And often the girls were very good sports. French Marie for example would let anyone have a tumble and when she fell pregnant the boys once again did the noble and right thing and drew straws to determine fathership. Sweets won this time and followed French out to the Cook Islands were he lived in a corrugated metal shack on a tropical beach. A strange move the boys thought for an asthmatic albino with psoriasis. When Little Legs married Nearly New Lulu he asked Big Nose and Ix if some of his mates, old army and travelling and drinking buddies, could crash at Number 9. The boys looked at the bodies of people they hardly knew lying across the floor and said they didn't understand the question. Legs and Lulu had the wedding at the golf club. It went very well, although they missed Jez and Bassy and Knob and Campbell the best man who had been lost and left in Calais during the stag night. And at the end of the wedding three of the Woodford Wimps pinched golfing buggies to try to get back to London on the cheap. When Legs got back from the honeymoon, a week in Amsterdam, drugs and hookers included, gifted by a drunk and generous Fatty Belly, (Legs had had to go on his own because Lulu, a promising stripper and clever girl, had already had enough,) most of his mates were still there. Most of his mates were still there two months later. That was Number 9, Lionfield Terrace, that was.

at the fish counter

a week after you died I saw you at the fish counter in Tesco's buying Haddock fillets and Conwy mussels, I said your name and reached out to touch your hair but stopped when I saw the look of concern on his wife's face

two weeks after you died I saw you walking the town walls wearing your long riding coat and Australian bush hat, you were walking quickly and with purpose, like Jesse James, I sounded the horn and waved but you didn't wave back so I drove around to the harbour where I thought you would come down, but you didn't

three weeks after you died I woke to find you sitting on the end of my bed, you were smiling, I asked you if you were ok and you nodded, and you put your thumb up, and you smiled again, and then I closed my eyes for a moment and when I opened them you were gone

that was the last time I saw you

and I wish you would come back

because I miss you

I really miss you

The Mallorca transcript

or the inane ramblings of 3 fifty something wannabe touring cyclists

P: My dear boys it looks something like this;
    Flight from Liverpool to Mallorca=£140 each
    Bike hire, Aluminium road bikes=100E each
    Car hire, 2 drivers, fully comp=£100 each
    Car park at Liverpool=25each
    Let me know what you girlies think.

B: Book it Danno.

P: I will need your passport details and your height in metres so I can get the right sized bikes.

G: Been in tedious meetings all day. The idea of flying off for a cycling trip with chums has never been so appealing. I'll send metric height and passport details ASAP.

P: Great. I'll book it all in the morning.

G: My height is1.8669mtrs (6' 2')

B: How the fuck do I know how tall I am you pair of cunts.

G: You will be around 14 hands.

P: I can tell you how fat you are if that helps.

G; Will there be a fat git premium for B?

P: I'm hoping after he has done a bit of exercise the plane will be considerably lighter on the way back and SleazyJet will give us a refund. Send;
    Passport details
    Full name
    DOB
    Girth
    Knob size
    Prospects

G: Knob size: adequate, just. Girth: significantly less than B's. Prospects: diminishing….

B: I'm glad you have admitted your knob size is significantly less than mine you loser.

G: Waist girth you twat.

P: You have both sent amusing, if childish, comments. However G is the only one who has sent me the details I require to book the trip (on my own, with my money, with no help.) So, pretty please, with bells on, get a fucking grip BeauroBoy.

B: How in God's name do I know how many cm tall I am. I suppose I am 5′ 8′ or 5′ 9′. Anyway stop bothering me with trivia, I have my public to take care of.

P: Trivia? It's for the frame size of your bike. Right, sod you then you're having a tricycle.

B: I want one bigger than yours but not as big as that lanky streak of piss.

G: Get him a clown outfit to go with his trike.

P: This is already a disaster. It's like going away with a couple of retards. I already feel like I am your carer.

B: Abuser

G: Who's going to bring the baby oil?

B: I think my existing frame is a 17′ — thanks, Dad.

G: Same size as my willy.

P: I need the tubby lad's DOB too. If you don't know your frame size you can measure it or google frame sizes and put in your height. Frame sizes go from 48 to 62, Take your time though boys because I've got naff all better to do than hang around waiting for you to get back to me. Alternatively, there is a sticker on the downside of your bike that will tell you. Mine, for example, is 54cm. D'you want a bell with your trike B?

B: I think mine is the same as yours. DOB 17/03/63.

P: That is not an answer. Read the sticker and get back to me. Now, for God's sake do some paper clipping.

G: You can rent bikes in Villafranca which is close to Manacor on the way to Porto Cristo.

P: Thank you so much for your input. However, I have already dismissed this company as too expensive and engaged the services of a better company who will deliver the bikes to our accommodation. They are merely awaiting my instructions as to the fucking sizes of the said bikes for Christ's sake.

G: I am a healthy 56cm in a road bike. Thanks for all the hard work in organising this, Dad. Has B been able to provide you with his full name yet?

B: Get me the same size as you.

P: Right, I will order 2x54cm and 1x58cm bikes.

G: Maybe a 56 for me, Dad (if there's a choice) although 58 would be ok. Ta, Dad.

B: Are you sure? You're more than 2cm taller than me.

G: Oh yeah. 56 then.

B: Are you sure?

G: 57?

P: They don't do a 57. They do a 56 or a 58. For fuck's sake make a decision.

G: ... oooh, 56. Oh, and see if you can get B a pendant flag on the end of a pole with the word 'wanker' written on it.

G: Sorry about that last text. Don't know what came over me. Gone and alienated myself now.

P: Right, I have ordered the bikes. As to your behaviour I am very disappointed in the pair of you. Your rudeness to me and to each other is neither big nor clever. You have let me down, but, more importantly, you have let yourselves down. This cavalier attitude and rather flippant approach to life has got to stop. If I don't see a marked improvement in your attitude you will have to face the consequence. You cunts.

G: It was him.

B: Wasn't.

P: Are you happy with a VW van, bit more expensive but means we can carry the bikes around the island.

G: Don't forget a car seat for B.

P: A booster should do it.

B: Go for it. Book it Danno.

P: You, B, are mistaking me for one of your retarded minions. And your delegation skills are laughable. You fucking go for it CuntyBollocks.

B: Car hire is the same as a packet of paper clips to me. I am a beaurocrat. I am strategic.

P: You are not strategic. You are a fat git. I will do it though otherwise we'll end up with one of those clown cars.

B: Parp Parp.

P: Jesus wept.

B: Honk Honk.

G: He's teasing you Dad.

B: There is a JP Donleavy story where a man meets an old friend who throughout the dialogue only says parp parp. It is quite sad. I suppose it must be an allegory or something. Parp Parp.

P: That is an interesting anecdote. The subtext of which is, 'you do everything because I am too cultured and sophisticated and fat and decadent and lazy to help.'

G: Best description of B I have ever heard.

B: Just book the car you mindless insect dullards. You are manual workers. Manual cunts.

P: Manual Cunts is the bloke we're renting the bikes off.

G: Ta Da.

P: Everything is booked. Where's my fucking money?

B: What money?

P: Now, do you boys need me to send you a list of things to pack?

B: Nope!! Cuddly donkey, sombrero and condoms is all I need.

G: Get him a list P else he'll be cadging from us.

P: So let me get this right B. You intend to have precautionary sex, wearing a sombrero, with a stuffed donkey?

B: I'll be on my hols, what's the issue?

P: At least you've set your sights on something achievable. And where's my fucking money you tight-fisted free-loading bastards.

B: Sorry, promise to pop around, away tonight. Very poor show on our part. But you are still a cunt.

G: Apologies P. Send me your bank details. I'll do a transfer.

P: Only joshing G. Sort it when I get back from The Smoke. It was B I was worried about. He's always been a bit of a chancer.

G: I know. He still owes me money. I didn't want to be tarred with the same brush.

P: He's never paid for anything.

G: Fucking liability.

P: Just back from London. £40 for 3 drinks. Gotta love 'em. The poppies were nice though. Gay but nice. Now where's my fucking money?

G: Do you do credit options ... I was thinking £10 per month?

P: Sorry G but no, I have a lifestyle to maintain and the compound interest on the amount you already owe me is significant and growing. You both have my bank details.

B: Did you polish your medals?

P: Did you polish your bell end?

B: For the full two minutes. Anyway, what's wrong with a cheque?

P: I simply haven't the time to deposit a cheque. I am far too busy pottering and writing poetry.

B: And I have a sophisticated bureaucracy to administer.

G: I have sent some wedge to you via the power of modern internet technology. Let me know if you get it.

B: I'm afraid I don't appear to have the power of modern internet technology. I shall write out a bill of exchange and as bearer of the same you may cash it against the promise implied therein.

P: See what I mean G? See what he's like?

G: Avoidance. By the way did you get the first instalment?

P: What?

G: Would you mind, old boy, checking your bank account for a small deposit made on Monday?

P: A small fucking deposit. What are you some kind of spermatozoa donor. Just tell me when the £264 you owe me has been paid in full. B, if you don't stop vacillating and pay up you will have to pay me in kind and enter your deposit in another fashion.

B: Gay.

P: Sorry if I was a tad brusque. All that talk of deposits inflamed me. I am a passionate man. And a holiday cottage magnate who simply hasn't the time to check his account for trifling sums. Now fucking pay up.

G: ...

B: ...

P: Oh dear, silence, I fear I am once again orbiting the Venn of friendship. Either that or you are both rushed off your feet doing important things with paper clips and staplers.

G: Too busy pushing a pen. I shall now send the full amount to the account you have specified.

B: You boys excited yet?

G: Yes, a growing excitement, tinged with the prospect of spending 10 days with anal cyclists wishing to flog a poor amateur. Go easy on me. I have been training though....I managed 1.5 miles last week.

B: I don't do anal.

P: I am fat and unfit and have asthma, so it's only that competitive twat B we'll have to worry about. Hopefully his gout will come back and slow him down.

G: We could knobble his effin tyres. Have you got your Euros yet. Dad?

P: Yes.

P: Perhaps you two will allow me to pay?

P: For everything.

P: Again.

G: The full amount has gone in.

P: Thanks. I'm running a writing course here this week. Lots of angst and creative paranoia. And that's only me. I'll be ready for cold beer, wine, brandy and tapas next week. Sod the cycling. And sod you too B, where's my fucking money?

B: Coming over tomorrow with a cheque. Aren't I G?

P: I'm not here. I will be with my writing people. And even if I was here I wouldn't want my clients to think that I'd stoop so low as to hang around with a couple of philistine uncreative pedestrian wankers like you two.

G: Don't worry P, we'll act like a couple of gay shirt lifters if your limerick students spot us.

B: Yeah. I'll staple your fucking cheque to one of them.

P: OK, that's fine, but please don't give the impression that you know me. Or engage them in any form of conversation.

G: Got insurance yet?

P: Yes, I have an annual family policy. Because I have been away from home before. You two, however, might be too old to be included on it. And fat.

G: I might pass for an Uncle. B for an aging grandparent.

P: You still ok to drive to the airport G.

G: Yup. Taking the Peugeot.

P: Oh dear.

G: Last day today. Must finish counting these paper clips and photocopying my arse.

B: My people will mourn me when I leave the Bureaucracy this afternoon.

P: Do we need sleeping bags? I don't mean in the Peugeot.

G: What?

P: Is there wifi? At the apartment I mean. Not in the Peugeot.

B: In Halfords now. Do we need anything? Puncture repair kit? Pump?

P: Hope. And faith.

G: Don't need sacks and there is wifi. Got a hell of an end day at work.

P: More filing? Nightmare.

B: Leaving Halfords. Boat missed.

P: See you in the morning. Don't be late.

B: Is there any plan at all? Remotely? A time corridor at least? You pair of non-communicative imbeciles.

P: Be at mine at 6:30.

B: If that is not a joke it is a logistical shambles. Remember we are dealing with G. His time doesn't converge with other time zones. You come to me for logistical sense. Not that idiot. It will be a disaster. He is a fucking liability.

P: Has anyone ever told you that you are very beautiful when you are angry?

B: Yes.

P: They lied.

G: I am here you know.

B: Yes, but you won't be there tomorrow.

G: I will. Did you say 8:30?

B: Oh God.

G: Can I take toothpaste on a plane?

B: I have pre-travel anxiety now.

G: I need a list. I need a fucking list.

P: Will you two be popping to the tip, like the gay lovers you are, before you pick me up?

G: Do you think we can fit it in B? I do have some debris.

P: Don't forget your cozzies.

B: Already packed. Don't be looking at me on the beach. In your funny way.

G: It's a nurses costume isn't it?

B: Navy.

P: What the fuck am I letting myself in for.

B: Sodomy.

P: Night, boys.

B: Sodomy.

G: Night, Dad.

reference poem

Peter is occasionally disruptive but largely just plain stupid.

Peter's contrition is wearing thin; along with another boy, he was discovered smoking in the cycle sheds, in full view of the road, by the Deputy Headmaster, when they should have been making their way to the second activity of the games afternoon. I wished to discuss Peter's attitude with Mr. Meade, our P.E. teacher, who stated simply, 'I do not know this boy.'

On his return to school after 'illness', I saw Peter and discussed with him at length our feelings about his behaviour and record of incidents, in and out of school; I was especially concerned about his frequent breaking of the rules, the ease with which he could express regret, and yet do the same thing again so readily. It is to be hoped that Peter can mature sufficiently to avoid 'putting his head in the noose' and to face up to his responsibilities, thus having no need to resort to false expressions of sorrow.

This is easily the best new collection of poetry I have read in years

I regret to inform you that as a result of a discussion between your son, Mr. Kemp the Training Superintendent and myself yesterday, Peter is no longer employed by this Company. Peter has received a number of warnings about his timekeeping, absenteeism and general conduct. I have agreed to pay Peter one week in lieu of notice as we feel that his presence on factory premises at this time would have an unfortunate and unfavourable effect on the other apprentices.

Gunner Marshall attained a very high level of skill in weapon handling. A tendency towards impulsive behaviour might diminish as he matures

Now that the School of Social Work's Child and Family elective is nearly finished and you have missed 60% of the sessions I am writing to tell you that you need not bother coming to the last two tutorials.

Marshall's writing combines a flamboyant Cavalier flair and panache with the Roundhead's common aggression and base brutality; he works very hard at his poetry and will go far.

Peter has a cavalier attitude to his profession and colleagues.

Thank you for your rather flippant response to our recent written warning. We stated that this was a first informal warning; you stated that you were 'Greatly looking forward to getting all dressed up for my first formal warning.' I must confess that the tone of your response did concern me somewhat but, nevertheless, I have added it to the relevant information on your file.

Pete and I have been married for over 30 years.

I must make it clear to you that the County Council and the ratepayers of Clwyd are entitled to expect high standards of conduct from it's Officers, and that in my view and that of Mr. Barnes, you have fallen far short of these standards.

Peter Marshall's poetry is incisive; like a scalpel, at first you feel nothing, and then, blood.

This company regards these matters in a serious light and regard your explanation concerning your poor time keeping, absenteeism and conduct as implausible in the extreme and evidence of your general unreliability, professional immaturity and cavalier attitude in ignoring agreed procedures.

Peter requires a clear format and simple guidelines as to the parameters of his responsibility and the expectations of his employer; if he gets these he is able to produce work that is barely adequate

I love my Daddy.

If you can get this man to work for you you will indeed be fortunate.

rugger

Cardiff;

a harmony of dragons and banners

of Gallic hordes in Mary Street

and there's Fast Eddie

a hobnailed grasshopper

rising from the skippering hulks
to study animals carved in castle stone

(he likes the lions

but knowing they can change
 is a trifle wary of the chameleons)

International Day

and there's Fast Eddie

jousting bustlers

yinning the yang
on rich ruby port

Grangetown Puking Cat Kung Fu

Alison Kraus

The cicadas stopped buzzing and the sound of the banjo blew in soft and sweet and slow on the breeze then hung languorous and eerily sensual in the spiralling smoke of their small fire before dissipating and rising spectral into the starry black satin sky.

'We should go see,' said one of the hunters.

'Yeah,' replied the other, shaking his head, 'and get fuckin' gut shot by some pissed up red-neck with a scatter gun.'

They sat in silence.

One of the men opened the cooler, plunged his hand deep into the ice and came up with a golden tin of Coors. He passed it to his friend, reached back in and pulled one for himself.

They leaned into the smoke and drank.

Scent of pine resin and sad cords of banjo music whispered through the wood interspersed with occasional shrieks. The hunters thought they heard the sound of chains being rattled.

One man stood. Then the other. They walked in the moonlight to the lakeshore following it along until they could see the fire. They made a lot of noise.

The music stopped.

When they were 100 yards out one of the men shouted. A voice answered telling them to come on in.

There were two men in the camp. One standing with his hands in his pockets, his gaunt and sunken features underlit and shadowy in the firelight. The other, a morbidly obese man with a high-domed bald head and cascading red beard sat like a malevolent Santa in a high backed leather armchair the stuffing of which protruded in places like the gutted intestines of a subdued beast. The banjo tucked neatly between two rolls of fat.

'Pass the shine Floyd,' the fat man said in a falsetto voice that didn't fit his frame, 'these boys might could be thirsty.' The man with the skeletal features reached across the fire, a clay jug hanging from a bony finger. One of the hunters took it and drank before passing it to his friend.

'Where y'all from boys?' the fat man asked, the firelight shiny on his greased and besmirched brow.

'Wales,' said one of the hunters.

'Say where?'

'Wales.'

The fat man shrugged. The skinny man giggled revealing a mouth entirely bereft of teeth.

'We're from the U.K.' said the other hunter.

'Ukraine?' enquired the fat man. The hunters said nothing. 'Don't make no never mind no how set boys we jes pickin' some 'n' yo welcome.'

The men sat.

The fat man looked over the fire at them and beyond into the dark forest. He cupped a hand to his mouth and shouted, 'Come up Darius.'

A rustle behind them caused the hunters to turn, a man shirtless and gleaming cadaverous and ghostly, the mirror image of Floyd, stepped forward, a pump action shot gun cradled in his skinny arms. He passed them, leaned the gun against a tree and stood hands pocketed next to Floyd, a bizarre mimic, only the whiteness of his bony torso to tell them apart.

The party sat silently drinking harsh bourbon whiskey from the cool clay jug.

The fat man leaned forward and gobbed a mouthful of liquorice coloured spit into the fire where it sizzled and bubbled in the embers. He lifted the banjo and strummed it twice.

Without warning and from somewhere behind him there came a demented groan and a pale creature leapt from the dark into the light. The hunters shuffled backwards away from the fire.

The child, for child it was, hurtled forward as if intent on jumping into the depths of the fire, only to be pulled up short and yanked off its feet by a length of chain secured by a manacle at its ankle. The child floundered barking and gibbonish on all fours in the dirt and the dust.

Floyd and Darius, seeing the discomfort of the two hunters, gibbered and shrieked and laughed and slapped their thighs. The fat man strummed the banjo seemingly oblivious; the strange boy on the chain found his feet and began a weirdly apelike pirouetting jig before the fire.

When the tune ended the fat man leaned forward and spat in the fire again. The boy stopped dancing, hobbled over to him and sat perched and gargoyle like on the arm of the chair while the fat man gently and with great care stroked the top of his head.

'Pay no mind to the chain boys,' the fat man whined, 'on accounta this crazed sonofabitch is liable to jes step right into that damned fire him bein' so dumb as to not even feel the pain till his skin's blistered and torn I know I seen it afore on a hot woodstove like this one time he cut loose 'n' cornered a skunk near the woodpile he started beatin' on that skunk with a ol' piece a two by four and each time he pops that damn skunk it sprays him and he jes keeps on beaten on it and him gittin' sprayed ever time God amighty I swear I ain't nary smelt nuthin' so bad nohow not even diggin' out a ol' cesspit which I done moren once him so bad Ma tried everthin' even to bathin' him in tomato juice didn't nothin' come close to curin' it holy goddamn shit.'

He patted the boy's head.

'You boys listen to bluegrass music where you from?'

The hunters nodded.

The fat man stretched his fingers and the knuckle bones popped loudly. 'Ya'll hear of a lil ol' girl name a Alison Kraus?'

The men nodded again.

'She used to sing in a Tennessee pickin' band a mine long time back she's my cousin voice like a goddamn angel and I tell y'all somethin' for nothin' the purtiest and sweetest piece a pussy I ever did taste I almost married her when she's say about near 15 guess the way things played out for her I damn well shoulda say what ya'll thinka that fellas?'

The hunters clicked their tongues and shook their heads in acknowledgement of the man's poor judgement and misfortune. Then they stood, nodded to all present, and took their leave.

'Alison Kraus,' they heard the fat man say, 'shit.'

At their camp the hunters replenished their fire. One reached into the cooler full of ice and pulled a beer. He handed it to his friend and reached in for one of his own.

The banjo sang and the chain rattled in the wood in the black American night.

They drank.

'Fuckin' hillbillies,' one said.

'You think?' said the other.

pacifists

the old soldier
listens carefully
to what the pretty hippie girl
has to say

sips his bitter

reaches over, takes her hand,

and tells her that

pacifists
aren't brave
they're
self-obsessed
cowards
who care about
nobody
but themselves

that pacifists
are deviants
who live outside
the morals
and mores
of society

that pacifists are deluded
(borderline psychotic)

that they hear voices

but not the pleas
of the child
victims
of aggression

that pacifists
shouldn't be allowed
to fight

that only the sane
and the brave
and the good

should go to war

Canvey

...so there's Campbell in Canvey working on the girls all night, asking them to dance buying them drinks trying to get his leg over all to no avail, they'd have the drink, of course, have a dance, maybe, and then walk away with somebody else better looking, same old Canvey Island Saturday Night Goldmine disaster, so now he's skint and the night's nearly over and he's at a loss and downtrodden and morose and therefore surprised when a fat girl comes over and tells him that she's been watching him all night and she thinks he's very handsome but also very sad because he'd no clue about how to pull a girl particularly not an Essex girl and she tells him that because she thinks he's cute she's going to give him one last chance and if he can find some new way to ask her for a date or whatever she would go with him and he thinks and thinks and she tuts and tuts and eventually looks at her watch and turns to walk away and he says no wait just give me one more minute and she turns and looks at him pityingly and says that was your last chance old lad and he tells her no wait listen do you fancy a shag to which she says no I fucking don't you cheeky bastard to which he says well darlin' would you mind lying down while I have one to which she says get your fuckin' coat kiddo you've bleedin' pulled...

Dull Knife

The following text came to light in the summer of 1996. A research student attached to the University of Oklahoma had been assigned the task of re-examining documentation kept in the Montana/ Nebraska historical society archives relating to the Battle of the Little Bighorn. Whilst examining a leather mail pouch, once the property of General E. Godfrey (a lieutenant serving with the 7th Cavalry at the time of the battle), she found Dull Knife's statement sown into the pouch's lining. The document has since been validated.

Although speculative, current opinion in the historical and archaeological community is that Godfrey, a long-standing supporter of Custer, hid the statement in an effort to perpetuate the myth of the 7th's (and therefore Custer's) gallant last stand. He sought to ensure that the legend, adopted by Custer apologists after the battle, of a cohesive military unit fighting bravely, shoulder to shoulder, to the last bullet and the last man was not undermined by Native American testimony.

Godfrey wanted to protect his regiment, the wives and families of the slain (including Custer's wife Elizabeth, a close personal friend of Godfrey's) and the memory of his beloved General.

The Custer myth suggests that what happened on that warm June day in 1876 day was inevitable; warriors drove brave soldiers to the final battleground, Custer Hill, a poor position but the best available militarily. There, desperately outnumbered, and with little chance of survival, the battalion formed a circle around their leader, and fought a glorious but doomed fight against the massed warrior hordes.

Dull Knife's testimony tells a different story. He lays the blame for the debacle squarely at Custer's feet. His account tells of a breakdown in tactical stability, which resulted in disintegration, panic, chaos, flight and bloody carnage; it is an account that mirrors current revisionist historical and archeological theories about the course of the battle.

Now I am an old man. But then I was young and strong and free. You whites have taken everything from the Indian. Our land is stolen. The buffalo are gone. You have murdered our chiefs in your jails. You massacred the last of my band at Wounded Knee. The Sioux tribe is scattered. The sacred hoop is broken. All I have left to me now is my life and I willingly offer it to you. I wish you would take it.

You Godfrey, you big soldier chief, you are a liar. I have heard your lies. You lied to your people and to the Great Father in Washington. You have said that the Custer soldiers fought well. That they were brave. That is a lie. They did not fight well. They ran from us. You lied about how we killed them and with your lies you stole the last of our honour. You stole our victory.

Indians have not told the truth about the fight because they thought that the white man would punish them for it. But I am no longer afraid. I will tell the truth and then I will die.

It was a big village. Many Indians. Many lodges. Many bands. Sans Arcs, Blackfeet Sioux, Cheyenne, Ogallala, Hunkpapa, Minneconjous, Two Kettles. The soldiers came during the day. It surprised us. Usually the soldiers attacked at sunrise. We thought we were safe because we were so many. I think they came in the day because they thought we would run away.

We fought the first soldiers in the valley. Women ran in screaming soldiers are coming. Soldiers killed a boy called Little Wolf. Killed two of Buffalo Hump's wives and his children. Warriors took weapons and went to meet them. At first soldiers rode in a line charging. Small flags flying. But when they saw how many we were they got off their horses and stood in a line shooting. They could not shoot straight. Warriors brought ponies and we rode out going fast to get behind them. Soldiers scattered like quail and ran into the timber near the river. Only one stayed behind. An Indian, an Arikara, a scout, an old enemy. He was very brave. He sang his death song and waited. Many warriors counted coup on him. Then killed him slowly with lances. We crushed his face with rocks. We could not get into the timber to kill the soldiers. Only two were killed on the flats. I saw two young men, Standing Bear and

Swift Elk, killed wastefully trying to charge the soldiers in the timber. The soldiers were safe there but did a strange thing. We heard the soldier chief shouting, then the soldiers charged out of the timber trying to get away. It became a great chase. Like a buffalo hunt. The soldiers went crazy. Firing their guns in the air. They were wild eyed like frightened deer. We chased them into the river and killed many of them as they tried to cross. I pulled one off his horse and killed him with my war club. I opened his belly and his guts floated in the river like weeds. Some climbed a high hill to get away. Some got left behind in the timber. Then we heard shooting from the village and knew more soldiers had come so went back to fight them.

A shirt wearer was telling the old men to take the women and children away because more soldiers were coming. I heard shooting further along. I went to my lodge to make medicine. My mother and father were there. I told them how many I had killed and showed them the scalps. My mother told me I had fought enough. She brought me food. My father told me I could rest. But I wanted to kill some more soldiers. I sang and made good medicine to stop the soldier bullets from hurting me. I painted my face blue and red. Put on my war bonnet. My father brought my best warhorse from the pony herd. I painted him. Hands and lightning. I took my Pawnee bone whistle. I told my father to take my mother away from the river in case more soldiers came. I took my new guns I had taken from the dead soldiers in the river fight.

In the next camp I met many Ogallala warriors painted and ready for war riding around and around. Bad Light Hair and White Eagle told me that their chief Crazy Horse had made a strong medicine to help kill the soldiers and I should ride with them. Our warriors and chiefs had fought the whites many times. We knew how they fought and we were ready for them. I think Custer was a fool. He attacked us before he knew how many we were. He killed his men for nothing. Indians would not have attacked against such numbers.

I decided to go with the Ogallala. We went to a shallow place. Warriors told us that soldiers had tried to cross here but had been fought back. Indians crossed this ford. Many Indians all going quickly up the ravines and coulees out of sight to fight the soldiers on the bluffs. I could hear the soldier guns going pop pop pop above not too fast at first and not too many. More Indians crossed the river and moved up to the soldiers. We left our ponies and crept closer hidden in the sagebrush and grass. They were in a line shooting down at us. Then some other soldiers on horses charged down amongst us. At first we ran back but a chief called Lame White Man shouted Hokahey it is a good day to die come young men fight and be brave. He charged the soldiers and we followed shooting fast into the horse soldiers from all sides. We pulled soldiers from their horses and the others started to gallop back up to their friends.

Things happened very quickly after the soldiers had charged down the hill. We ran after them. Some of the soldiers at the top were not shooting. They were holding the horses of the soldiers who were shooting. Someone said we should kill the horse holders and stampede the horses which we did. Then the soldiers could not get away. They gathered in bunches all on top of each other and we killed them easily. Further up on a ridge other soldiers had gathered. A lot. All in a big bunch. Indians on all sides shooting into them. Indians charged in and killed them with knives and clubs.

We had fought Custer before at the Washita. He did the same there. Sending his soldiers in different groups. At the Washita he captured our women and children so that we could not fight him.

From where we had killed the bunch of soldiers I could see another lot of soldiers a long way off. On their horses. All in a line. Just waiting. I think they were waiting for other soldiers to come so that they would be stronger. Custer did not know that we had already killed many of the other soldiers in the river fight and those we had not killed were hiding on top of a hill a long way away. They were frightened. Those soldiers would not come to help him.

Soldiers now were running along the ridge in ones and twos to try I think and get to the soldiers who waited further over in lines. Indians chased them on either side. Some of the soldiers had thrown away their guns and just ran. Others just fired their guns in the air while they were running. We chased them and killed a lot more on the ridge. One soldier, a chief I think, was riding a pretty horse with four white socks. He was very brave. He kept charging back into the Indians so that his friends could run away. All the Indians wanted his horse. He fought well until all his bullets were gone and then charged with a big knife. He was killed with arrows. He was wearing a pale buckskin jacket. After the fight we left his body alone because he was so brave.

Another soldier chief on a pretty horse tried to get away. He galloped away and was chased by three Indians. But his horse was fast and they could not catch him so they stopped. Then the soldier did a strange thing. He drew his small gun and shot himself. I do not know why he did that.

After a while the soldiers who waited in lines further away got chased up the hill by more Indians. The Cheyenne had crossed the river at the other end of the village. These soldiers went to the highest hill and met the last of the soldiers from the ridge. Indians were all around them now sneaking up in the prairie grass to get close. There were many Indians below the soldiers on the high hill as well. A group of soldiers on nice grey horses charged down the hill into those Indians. At first the Indians ran back again but then a Chief, Bloody Axe I think, told them to be brave so the warriors turned and charged the soldiers killing many. Those soldiers not killed went back up to their friends. These last soldiers on the high hill killed their horses and hid behind them. Some fired at the Indians but not all. All around them Indians crept closer and closer. A Sans Arc, Grey Moon, was next to me. He would stand and shoot and then duck back down until one time he stood and a soldier bullet hit him in the middle of his forehead and he fell dead.

Near the end of the fight some soldiers did a strange thing. A big bunch stood up and ran down the hill. I think they were trying to get away. They were very wild and excited. Like crazy people. Some shot their guns into the air. They ran as if they had been drinking whiskey. Arms going around and around. Some left their guns behind. We chased them into a deep cut in the hill with steep banks and killed them by shooting down into them. They could not get out. Some Indians jumped in and killed them with knives. Some soldiers hid in the long grass and pretended to be dead but we found them and killed them. Some soldiers were foolish and threw their guns down and put their hands in the air and cried. We laughed at them and killed them. On the hill the soldiers stopped firing and Indians charged in and killed them all. The fight did not take long.

I think Custer lost this fight because he thought we would run away. He sent soldiers to attack the village at one end. He sent other soldiers to attack the village at the other end. And he sent soldiers to attack the village in the middle. Like at the Washita. But the village was too big. The distance too great. His soldiers were too few and not brave. He should have seen this. An Indian would have seen it. He should have run away.

After the fight we stripped the soldiers and took their guns and bullets. Some of the soldiers had not shot any bullets. A lot of the soldiers had killed themselves with their own guns. I don't know why. Women and children came up from the village. Warriors took the soldier scalps and pierced the soldier bodies with lances. The women cut off their ears and noses. They plucked out their eyes. They cut off their hands and feet and heads and genitals. They pushed arrows into their penises. They smashed their faces and cut out their intestines and threw them all around all mixed up.

Indians found a lot of green paper on the soldiers. All of the soldiers had it. Indians threw it in the air and it floated away. Later I saw a child making a pony out of river clay. He used one of the papers for a saddle blanket.

Many warriors rode off to kill the soldiers left from the river fight but I was tired and went back to my tipi to sleep. That night we had a big dance. We gave two soldiers we had caught to those too young to fight. One soldier had black skin. Sioux boys skinned him alive and filled a kettle with his blood slowly. They set small fires under the other. He took a long time to die and was not brave. I went from camp to camp to dance with the girls. It was a good feast.

The next day I went to see my friend Bear Tooth. He had been shot in the belly by a soldier. He lay quiet. Looking up. He wanted water but his father said it would kill him. He said to his mother he wished he could have some water but she looked away. I felt sad because I knew he would die. There was nothing I could do so I told him he had been brave and went away.

The next day I went to kill some of the soldiers on the other hill. They had dug holes in the earth to hide in like prairie dogs. They shot well. It was hard to get near them. We shot at them from a ridge. We had a lot of soldier bullets. I think we killed some but not many. Hawk Man, Long Robe and Dog Back were killed there. They wanted to count coup but the soldiers saw them and killed them.

Not many warriors were killed in the Custer fight. Those killed were dressed in their finest clothes and left with their

60

weapons on buffalo robes in two tipis. Later we heard that other soldiers were coming. The great camp moved away to the Bighorn Mountains and there the bands went their different ways.

I have spoken the truth.

Immediately after the battle military sources, including Lieutenant Godfrey, claimed that Indian fatalities were very heavy, that the bodies of the warriors had *'piled up like cordwood,'* so effective had been the firing of the soldiers.

The 7th Cavalry lost 260 men. Of the troopers who rode into battle under the direct command of George Armstrong Custer there were no survivors. Most historians now agree that one of Custer's prime objectives at the Little Bighorn was to prevent hostile savages from fleeing the area in order to fight another day.

Dull knife starved himself to death after making his statement. The cause of death entered into the reservation's medical register stated that he had died from   'a prolonged bout of melancholia.'

John Eagle Feather,
Tribal Historian and Lakota Elder,
Sheridan, Wyoming,
20th April 2005.

The Old Poetry

for Peter Brown

He dum de dum de dum de dum de dum de dum de haughty,
He dum de dum de dum de dum de dum de dum de naughty;

She dum de dum de dum de dum de dum de dum de moor
She dum de dum de dum de dum de dum de dum downpour;

She dum de dum de dum de dum de dum de dum de chill,
She dum de dum de dum de dum de dum de dum de ill;

He dum de dum de dum de dum de dum de dum remorse,
He dum de dum de dum de dum de dum de dum recourse;

He dum de dum de dum de dum de dum de dum sick bed,
She dum de dum de dum de dum de dum de dum de dead.

the new poetry

nudge
the comma
the colon
nudge
the bracket
say
no in
inverted
commas
more is less
punctuated
a postraphe
nods
as a donkey
dash hyphen
derbys a
good buy
2 all that
as emi
colons
      a
wink
2 rongs
dontmake
a rite
a full
stopsa
blind
upper alley
bat
exclamation
mark s
      n
spensers
meals
r nice

Budapest

Even though his kids had grown up and moved away and had their own relationships he loved them so much that he wanted to manufacture situations that would enable him to spend time with them. On this occasion he had talked his two boys, who were now men, into going on a cycle trip with him from England to Budapest. It would be a great experience for them. They would get fit and it would be a great physical achievement. They could raise money for charity. And the trip would be his treat. He would get the beer.

He talked his wife, who didn't really fancy the cycle, into renting an apartment and meeting them in Budapest at the end of the cycle trip. It was agreed and arranged. A big family adventure.

The cycle trip went well. They started in Calais and cycled to the Rhine and then on to the Danube. They did about 70 miles a day. He pushed them, but he didn't push them too hard. He wanted them to have a good time. He hoped that they would like it and do it again sometime. As long as they got to Budapest when their mum arrived that would be fine.

They drank beer every night and ate good food. They partied heavily in a couple of towns, especially in Germany and Austria, and especially along the Danube in Regensburg and Passau and Linz and Vienna. And he noticed something when they had finished cycling and were out for the evening. He noticed that, although they loved him, and liked his company, they also wanted their own space to party like the young men they were, to smoke dope and chase girls and do young man stuff.

The boys wouldn't have said anything to him. They loved him and wouldn't have wanted to hurt his feelings. But he spotted it himself. So he started staying out with them until about 10pm and then he would feign tiredness, he would tell the boys that he needed an early night and make his excuses and, after giving them some beer money, head back to the tent or hotel.

And he would lie in his tent and wait. And then he would fall asleep because, as he suspected, when he wasn't there the boys got on with the things young men got on with and stayed out partying until the wee small hours, heading off on their morning cycle with appalling hangovers.

He wouldn't let them off the cycle because, he told them, they had to be there to meet their mum. But he was glad that they were having a good time and were bonded as brothers.

They got to Budapest three days before his wife was due to arrive and took over the apartment. They had a good time exploring the city and eating out and at night he went drinking with them in some of the great bohemian bars until about 10pm and then he left them to their own devices.

He'd take a slow walk back to the apartment stopping off for a few glasses of palinka on the way. On the night before his wife was due to arrive he stopped off at one bar and ordered his palinka. He turned and leaned against the bar looking out at the people seated around the place and his eyes rested upon a beautiful young girl who was sitting on her own staring back at him.

She smiled at him and he smiled back raising his glass and then turned back to the bar.

A few moments later the girl came and sat on the bar stool next to him. He turned and saw that she was not only beautiful, she was stunningly beautiful, with very pale skin, delicately chiselled cheekbones, a fine sharply angular nose, large brown doe like eyes and long jet black hair which she had tied up in a ponytail.

She was, he thought, the second most beautiful girl he had ever seen.

She reached out and took his hand.

'English?' She asked.

'Yes,' he said.

'Welcome to Budapest.'

'Thank you.'

'You like here?' She stared intently into his face, into his eyes.

'Very much,' he said, 'I love it.'

'Ah, love,' she said smiling, not letting go of his hand, 'you would like to make some love with me I think? Some good sex time. Yes. Some good sexy time with me. Not expensive.'

His mouth opened but he couldn't speak.

She laughed.

'So,' she said, 'what you think? I am pretty no?'

He smiled at her. And stared into her eyes.

'Yes,' he said, 'you are very pretty. How old are you?'

'It doesn't matter. Not too old. 21. Why?'

'Well,' he said, 'you are very lovely and I am honoured that you would ask me this but I am too old for you and I am married and you are the same age as my daughter. So, of course, I am very tempted by your kind offer, but I think it would be wrong for me to say yes. I'm sorry.'

'Ok,' she said, shrugging her shoulders, 'it doesn't matter. Would you like to spend some time with me anyway? You can buy me a drink and I can practise my English.'

'I'd like that a great deal. It would be a pleasure. What can I get you to drink? And what's your name? I'm Mark.'

'I'm Adriana. No drink here. I work here. I have to pay them. Let's go over the river. To my place. It's better. Full of music. You will like.'

So they took a cab to the Gypsy quarter and drank and sang and danced and he met her family and he got hugged and kissed by giant men with huge moustaches and they talked until the night had gone and he asked her why she did what she did because she was as clever as she was beautiful and she told him that she was a Gypsy and that a Gypsy had three ways to live; to beg, to rob and steal, or to whore and she told him that she was too proud to beg and too honest to steal so she had decided to whore.

The tale she told made him decide to tell her about his daughter. About why she wouldn't be flying out to Budapest with his wife. A story, he said, he hadn't told anybody else. He brushed her cheek, then took the girl's hand and told her that his daughter, who was the most beautiful girl he had ever seen, had become addicted to drugs at an early age, cannabis to start with and then heroin. She had left home when she was 17. She had turned to prostitution when she was 19 to support her habit. And he told the girl that he had made the decision not to help his daughter financially because he thought it was the right thing to do. Because he didn't want to encourage her. And he told the girl that his daughter had died of an overdose when she was 21. That she had died alone. Far away from her family. And he told the girl about how much he missed his daughter and about how much he had loved her.

They sat holding hands in silence for a long time. And when he said he had to go they embraced and wept and told each other they would never forget this night and would never forget each other.

On his slow walk back through the streets the man wept again and wondered if his daughter would have been coming to Budapest with his wife if he had acted differently. If he had supported her financially. If he had taken better care of her. And he knew that his wife would be wondering the same thing on the flight over.

He got back at the apartment long after the boys.

a shorts text

P: Alright, son?

D: Alright, dad.

P: You busy?

D: I'm in work aren't I so of course not.

P: Good lad, I'll crack on then. I have a new radical right wing pen-pal from Colorado. You will be very jealous, she is very beautiful, carries a concealed hand gun, wants to put a fence up around California and along the Rio Grande and can wear a cowboy hat without irony. Her family are visiting in June if you fancy giving them a guided tour of Oxford.

D: Love to. She sounds cool.

P: She also thinks I am full of shit and a liberal.

D: You are full of shit.

P: Yes, but not a liberal.

D: You haven't been on those websites again have you?

P: What websites?

D: Those websites for sad lonely old degenerates.

P: Don't call her that. She is my new girlfriend.

D: Not her, you, you twat. And she is not your girlfriend.

P: Why not?

D: Because you are like a thousand years old. Who is she then?

P: Like I said they're coming on holiday. Got chatting. Swapped photos etc.

D: You sent her a photo of you?

P: Yup.

D: And she replied? What is she, a blind American?

P: No, I sent her a photo of me in my shorts and she fell for me.

D: Fainted from shock more like? What shorts?

P: My cut offs.

D: Oh for fuck's sake, Dad. You are joking. They were obscene 10 years ago. You'll cause an international incident? Please for everything sane tell me you don't still wear them.

P: I am a fine figure of a man and you should have more respect for your father's thighs. Anyway, we got talking about Baltimore and I wondered what you reckon about the situation out there.

D: It's shite.

P: In a little more detail perhaps, Sherlock.

D: Baltimore is a reaction to a young black man who 'died' in police custody, a wider pattern of young black men killed by the police which really kicked off with Michael Brown in Ferguson. Dozens have been killed since then and friggin' thousands in the last ten years. More than Brit casualties in Afghan and Iraq. It's also about poor disenfranchised black areas right next to wealthy white areas with mostly white cops. Also, U.S. police forces appear to have been massively militarised since 2001, surplus weapons plus loads of vets. More machine guns than the British Army. Police taking hard action during riots against shootings of unarmed black lads by white coppers; think Belfast in the early 70s.

P: Cheers.

D: You've bloody got me started now, I've been following this with interest. Seems to me its basically like the battle of the Bogside. Police and communities opposed, big sectarian/racial divide. Police seen as hostile outsiders. Reminds me a lot of how the Republicans saw the R.U.C. and B Specials.

P: Cheers. I'm going to send this to my new girlfriend to show her what a clever boy you are. Although she thinks they are bloated and lazy black men on welfare who breed with as many different women as possible and that the women who have their children are lazy feckless sluts on welfare.

D: She is not your girlfriend and you're a deluded and patronising old fool. She is clearly a bigoted, myopic and racist fruit loop.

P: Oh dear. But she is very attractive.

D: So was Hitler.

P: No he wasn't.

D: He was to Eva. Who was also deluded.

P: I'll make you eat those words when I leave you far behind on our cycle trip. I demand some respect. I am your father and I used to wipe your bottom. Need to meet for beer ASAP?

D: Sounds good, I'm on me tod this weekend, if you're up for it?

P: Can't this weekend. Making more shorts.

D: Jesus wept!

P: See you soon, mate. Take care.

D: And you.

Tazzer

At the Urdd Eisteddfod frantic teachers panic like flushed quail, herd their flocked charges too and from the podium, bemused incomers view the same skits over and over and over again, watch their children sing songs and recite poems with pained expressions on their gurning faces like little angels with belly ache, and at the back of the hall Tazzer, from Toxteth, importer of exotic flowers, drug dealer and sometime paratrooper is wired into his I-Pod watching the man on the door holding it shut with a piece of binder twine, the man will not let anybody in or out of the hall, not while there's a performance on, it is more than his job is worth, he shakes his head impassively at the little girl who desperately needs the toilet, Tazzer keeps watching, watches the man's cold stare, watches him raise a finger to his lips to hush the little girl who is pleading with him to be let out, watches as the child clutches herself but cannot stop the urine from running down her legs, Tazzer, perhaps mistaking culture for cruelty and tradition for torture bides his time, follows the man along school corridors lined with dragon art and daffodils to the toilets, nuts him into the cubicle [*shattered proboscis spraying snot, blood and gore*] takes out his cock and sprays a frothy stream of Jagermeister and Red Bull inspired piss over his sharply pressed moleskin trousers, leans forward to admonish the chap, 'Ow d'you fuckin' like it eh lah, ow do you fuckin' like it you fuckin' nasty fuckin' nazi bastard, culture is it eh lah, I'll give you fuckin' culture.'

Jester

The dull thud of broken paving slabs and the soft liquid whoosh of the Molotov cocktails hitting their armoured vehicle tells the soldiers that they have arrived. On the order to dismount they clamber out into a grey and derelict scene of urban devastation as wild and grim and forbidding as any wolverine plagued Yukon landscape.

Under a barrage of stone and glass they form up in lines behind their macrolon shields, the enemy facing them a fearful and rabid prospect, the scene more reminiscent of wars past than of any 20th Century confrontation.

The Fenian crowd yammering and baying for blood sing their rebel songs and lob half house bricks high into the air to fall onto the soldiers taking cover behind their defensive screen.

The soldiers after their own fashion pound their shields with their three-foot long wooden truncheons and fire baton rounds low so that they bounce in front of the crowd to strike shins and vulnerable genitalia.

The adversaries shift too and fro, side to side, probing wave-like, parrying turn and turn about, taunting each other as the Roman legionnaires and barbarian Vandals must have in an early Germanic conflagration.

And behind the mayhem a terraced house in flames.

A woman of a different tribe. A mother, tearing her hair and beating her breast. Crying for her babies. Pleading for help from her god and from the impotent fire and ambulance crews denied access by the rioting mob.

In the middle of the fray, in the front rank of soldiers, standing head and shoulders above his brothers-in-arms a black man from another city and another continent throws his shield and cudgel to the ground and lets out an unearthly bellow loud enough to silence the chants of the crowd and the relentless drumming of the uniformed men.

The black soldier walks forward in this weirdly conjured and unearthly silence until he stands equidistant between the combatants.

From somewhere at the back of the crowd a jagged piece of roof slate hisses through the still morning air and the smoke and cuts across the black soldier's forehead. He falls to his knees, the blood running messiah-like down his face, and raising his hands to heaven bellows once more in his rage and his frustration and his blind primitive fury.

He falls forward again so that his hands rest on the broken tarmac. His blood drips audibly. The very ether around him shimmers, crackles like static electricity, smells of ozone and for a brief animistic moment he looks to those present for all the world like some great holy warrior of the dark African savannah, like some displaced Maasai Chieftain, lordly and regal, and then he blows through pursed lips and bellows again into the quiet street.

Wearily he finds his feet and very slowly raises a finger to point, like some somber judge, a warning, first at the subdued crowd in their mismatched and ill-fitting clothes, and then, turning, points again at the lines of uncertain men in their starched combat uniforms.

With great deliberation, as if a huge weight is pressing down upon him, he walks toward the burning house and the crowd parts to let him through.

As he passes the screaming woman he touches her gently on the shoulder and her wailing subsides.

The black soldier walks through the door of the burning building and disappears into the billowing smoke only to re-appear minutes later carrying the grotesque, twisted and burnt bodies of the two little girls who had been in their beds when the device exploded.

He walks back toward the crowd holding his tiny burden in front of him with great care and reverence not unlike some ancient shaman carrying an offering to a pagan deity. And as he passes between the crowd and the soldiers he proffers the bodies for all to see druidic in his greenery and in his calm countenance and not at all accusatory.

Delicately he places the ruined bodies of the children into one of the waiting ambulances, returns to collect his shield and club, then climbs tired and clumsy into the back of his Saracen armoured car.

In an uncomfortable shuffling silence the raggedy crowd disperses.

Without instruction or any semblance of order the soldiers lower their shields and return to their vehicles.

On the way back to the rancid mill that is their current dwelling the soldiers, as men of courage *in extremis* often do, joke and laugh about things that they have seen. They nudge and shove each other and shout about how Stedroy Fenton, Jester to his comrades, had walked the line with an armful of twiglets, had walked the line with an armful of fuckin' twiglets.

But they do not talk about what really happened this day. They will not give it credence. Nor will they look at the tears on the face of the black soldier silently weeping in the shadows in the corner of the armoured car.

a long overdue I love you poem for Jacquie

Jag älskar dig Je t'aime Ich liebe dich Ti amo Eu te amo Я тебя
люблю Te amo Ik houd van u Σ'αγαπώ Jag älskar dig أنـا أحـبّ أنـت
Cara 'ch EGO diligo vos JEG elske jer ÉG ást þú I-KIRJAIN lempiä
te JEG elske du Volim te Szeretlek JA miłość ty JÁ Amor tebe АЗ
любов ти I dragoste tu JA ljubav te ljubim te محبت اپ سے مجھے Ben
seni severim من دوسـت دارم Tôi yêu bạn Mahal kita Seni seviyorum
Inħobbok Es mīlu Tevi Я тебе люблю Aš tave myliu Kocham cię Я
люблю Вас مـينه مـی تـاسـو I love you Jag älskar dig Je t'aime Ich liebe
dich Ti amo Eu te amo Я тебя люблю Te amo Ik houd van u
Σ'αγαπώ Jag älskar dig أنـا أحـبّ أنـت Cara 'ch EGO diligo vos JEG
elske jer ÉG ást þú I-KIRJAIN lempiä te JEG elske du Volim te
Szeretlek JA miłość ty JÁ Amor tebe АЗ любов ти I dragoste tu JA
ljubav te ljubim te محبت اپ سے مجھے Ben seni severim من دوسـت دارم
Tôi yêu bạn Mahal kita Seni seviyorum Inħobbok Es mīlu Tevi Я
тебе люблю Aš tave myliu Kocham cię Я люблю Вас مـينه مـی تـاسـو I
love you Jag älskar dig Je t'aime Ich liebe dich Ti amo Eu te amo Я
тебя люблю Te amo Ik houd van u Σ'αγαπώ Jag älskar dig أنـا أحـبّ
أنـت Cara 'ch EGO diligo vos JEG elske jer ÉG ást þú I-KIRJAIN
lempiä te JEG elske du Volim te Szeretlek JA miłość ty JÁ Amor
tebe АЗ любов ти I dragoste tu JA ljubav te ljubim te اپ سـے مـجهے
محـبت Ben seni severim ت دارم مـ ن دوس Tôi yêu bạn Mahal kita Seni
seviyorum Inħobbok Es mīlu Tevi Я тебе люблю Aš tave myliu
Kocham cię Я люблю Вас مـينه مـی تـاسـو I love you Jag älskar dig Je
t'aime Ich liebe dich Ti amo Eu te amo Я тебя люблю Te amo Ik
houd van u Σ'αγαπώ Jag älskar dig أنا أحبّ أنت Cara 'ch EGO diligo
vos JEG elske jer ÉG ást þú I-KIRJAIN lempiä te JEG elske du Volim
te Szeretlek JA miłość ty JÁ Amor tebe АЗ любов ти I dragoste tu
JA ljubav te ljubim te محبت اپ سے مجھے Ben seni severim من دوست دارم
Tôi yêu bạn Mahal kita Seni seviyorum Inħobbok Es mīlu Tevi Я
тебе люблю Aš tave myliu Kocham cię Я люблю Вас مـينه مـی تـاسـو I
love you Jag älskar dig Je t'aime Ich liebe dich Ti amo Eu te amo Я
тебя люблю Te amo Ik houd van u Σ'αγαπώ Jag älskar dig أنـا أحـبّ
أنـت Cara 'ch EGO diligo vos JEG elske jer ÉG ást þú I-KIRJAIN
lempiä te JEG elske du Volim te Szeretlek JA miłość ty JÁ Amor
tebe АЗ любов ти I dragoste tu JA ljubav te ljubim te اپ سـے مـجهے
محبت Ben seni severim من دوست دارم Tôi yêu bạn Mahal kita Seni

seviyorum Inħobbok Es mīlu Tevi Я тебе люблю Aš tave myliu
Kocham cię Я люблю Вас تاسو می مـینه I love you Jag älskar dig Je
t'aime Ich liebe dich Ti amo Eu te amo Я тебя люблю Te amo Ik
houd van u Σ'αγαπώ Jag älskar dig أنت أحبّ أنا Cara 'ch EGO diligo
vos JEG elske jer ÉG ást þú I-KIRJAIN lempiä te JEG elske du Volim
te Szeretlek JA miłość ty JÁ Amor tebe АЗ любов ти I dragoste tu
JA ljubav te ljubim te محبت سے اپ مجھے Ben seni severim من دوست دارم
Tôi yêu bạn Mahal kita Seni seviyorum Inħobbok Es mīlu Tevi Я
тебе люблю Aš tave myliu Kocham cię Я люблю Вас تاسو می مـینه I
love you Jag älskar dig Je t'aime Ich liebe dich Ti amo Eu te amo Я
тебя люблю Te amo Ik houd van u Σ'αγαπώ Jag älskar dig أحبّ أنـا
أنـت Cara 'ch EGO diligo vos JEG elske jer ÉG ást þú I-KIRJAIN
lempiä te JEG elske du Volim te Szeretlek JA miłość ty JÁ Amor
tebe АЗ любов ти I dragoste tu JA ljubav te ljubim te سـے اپ مـجھے
مـحبت Ben seni severim ت دارم ن دوس مـ Tôi yêu bạn Mahal kita Seni
seviyorum Inħobbok Es mīlu Tevi Я тебе люблю Aš tave myliu
Kocham cię Я люблю Вас تاسو می مـینه I love you Jag älskar dig Je
t'aime Ich liebe dich Ti amo Eu te amo Я тебя люблю Te amo Ik
houd van u Σ'αγαπώ Jag älskar dig أنا

naughty in the office random predicted text prose poem on my iPhone

...in the past tense easily the best thing in the anniversary of the world ever is when I get my hair done tomorrow is a very long time to see the whole world or not the whole world or to see what happens when I get to know how I can do it on a Friday afternoon in the morning and the whole time. The president of the year before the end zone and a half hour to write about a month or more to do that in my room for improvement but quickly and I have a lot more fun if I could have a great way of saying that the government has been the most recent quarter. A new phone is a good idea of a sudden urge to be able to see who has the best thing in the world ever. Even though the world is full of them in my life and death and destruction and the whole world is not an option for the next few weeks and months and the whole time I try to be a great way for the rest of the day before I go to Beddgelert and the whole thing is that I don't have a lot of fun with it...

love and romance in the vernacular

poem overheard from the floor of the gentlemen's urinals in The Oddfellows Arms, Chelmsford, Essex, circa 1981, while feeling slightly the worse for wear:

...driptrays on the piss, Fatty Belly Frosty, Sweets, Big-Nose, Ix, Suicidal Jez, Little Legs, Campbell, usual suspects, mob-handed, so they've taken their first casualty 9ish, Big Nose striped by a chink in The Empire, givin' it 'why for you kick my dog and call him fuck off,'

anyway

cut a long story short

thinkin' discretion's the better part they beat a hasty back to The Oddfellows, Fatty Belly's already given it 'oy Gunga three red stuffs,' and 'ad 2 Ticcas a Rogan and a Bombay Duck prior to the chinky so course he's fuckin' parched ain't he, dry as a dead dingo's donga,

anyway

cut a long story short

he only nominates fuckin' snakebites, causing the boys to give it large tryin' to keep up with him, always fuckin' rash as you very well know and by 9 they're shapeless watchin' Frosty prancin' about starkers with a packet of Cadbury's Smash dangling from his dick on a bit of string givin' it 'who's for bangers and mash then?'

anyway

cut a long story short

he's gettin' admirin' glances all round because as you know he's a tad fuckin' muleish in that department and winds up pullin' this fuckin' pikey slapper from Billericay who's been matching him pint for pint on the old Bob and Abbot who Leg's informs me later straight up is the mankiest tart he's ever clapped his minces on, never seen anything so ugly he reckons with only one head, like a fuckin' bull dog chewin' a wasp, and they all end up back at Ix's drum except Suicidal who's gone to his tree down the Bunny Walks to see if he fancies hangin' himself,

anyway

cut a long story short

turns out this pikey sort might have been slapped about with the ugly stick and a bloater to boot but she's also a fuckin' good sport and bish-bosh ends up lettin' 'em all have a tumble, bit like chuckin' a sausage down an alleyway by all accounts, still beggars and wotnot,

anyway

cut a long story short

couple a months later she only turns up down the Odds with a couple of fuckin' enormous pikeys in tow, I mean big fuckin' fuckers tattoos all over their mugs like a couple a fuckin' Commanches, turns out the pikey bint's up the duff and they have two choices a). do the honourable or

2). go down your traditional pikey route and end up tied to a tree in Epping Forest with your fuckin' bollocks in your chops, course the boys ain't slow and as one they 'ave it away on their toes out the back door only to find two more giant pikeys cradlin' fuckin' scatter guns outside,

anyway

cut a long story short

as you very well know some of the boys are fairly handy but they know as well as yours truly that you don't want a war with a bunch of fuckin' pissed off pikeys, not on a matter of family honour you fuckin' don't, so she gives 'em a week, and they meet in the snug next day,

Suicidal's there too, arm in plaster where he fell out of his tree, only he was too fuckin' shedded to remember whether he give her a tickle or not, he'd lose his fuckin' balls if they weren't in a bag, so they draw straws like you do and course he only pulls the short one,

anyway

cut a long story short

he only fuckin' marries her don't he and gets bought a tidy gaff in Broomfield by the pikey's brothers who've taken a shining to Jez's suicidal boat-race, she carves down, drops the sprog in Jez's lap and he only falls arse over tit for the little scrote, absolutely made up he is, fuckin' besotted, five years later they flog the gaff for

double the bunce, wack half of it in the Barclays and fuck off the 3 of 'em together to travel the world last anyone's heard of them they're living' in some fuckin' house on stilts in Borneo wherever the fuck that is, and I'll tell you somethin' for nothing my old China, if that ain't fuckin poetry my knobs a nana…..

Liverpool Maritime Museum.
Archive.

Aged five entered the workhouse with me mother where I was taken from her, sent to Indefatigable school ship for the destitute sons of sailors and orphans, learned there not to like bullies or misplaced authority and to fight me corner. Then to sea. Rounded the Horn before I was thirteen in the boom years of the San Francisco grain trade, coal from Liverpool out, grain back. Nitrate guano trade from Chile flourishing too. Sailed once with crew no mariner wants, the dross scum and worst criminal rogues Liverpool had to puke up, confronted with one such on fore watch tapped him with a pin 'till he fell poleaxed like a split mast onto the deck eyes white and rolled up into his skull, he went over next day. I'll say no more about that. Jumped ship in South America to avoid retribution deserved or otherwise. Bought the papers of a derelict and drunk seaman to resume me career as Hugh Forrester. April 1891 signed off the brigantine Isabella Walker, Burry port. December 1891 on the American four-masted schooner Edith Berwind, worked me passage home from Philadelphia aboard S.S. Helen. Used the name John Stevenson first, and thereafter. July 1892 aboard the Lord Charlemont bound for Baltimore. Christmas Day 1892 the Tropea bound for Galveston busted her shaft and put into Falmouth Harbour, a storm blew up because the cook hadn't peeled the spuds. We pelted him with veg and a paddy threw a knife, the peelers were called. Next day the crew, meself among them, refused to sail because of bad grub, all prosecuted and pleaded guilty but offered the chance to rejoin if we paid out our expenses. Declined and was sentenced to three weeks hard labour in Bodmin Gaol. Sailed in the Provincia from Blythe, a hard man I was by then, but not without talent. 1895 promoted Bosun and Lamptrimmer on the Bencliff aged only 22. Sailed the Birdoswald a meandering voyage along the Indian coast, she not being a happy ship many of the crew signed off in sub-continental ports along the way, even the mate went ashore. One time anchored near Cochin in the wet and sticky monsoon six and a half weeks tempers fraying the master being rude and belligerent I was forced to knock him down. Found guilty of assault by the port authority in Colombo given one month's rigorous imprisonment. May 1899 signed aboard the

Warwick as Bosun and Lamptrimmer, paid to stand by her during the building to watch over the owner's interests. Sailed on the Leafield for Canadian owners thinking it a delivery voyage only, crew kept aboard under duress to trade the Great Lakes, jumped ship in Detroit, stowed back to Liverpool on a Yankee. Signed on the Basil for coasting 1901. Signed on the Kittie of Hartlepool February 1902. Got wed 18th November 1907 after a visit from the priest, her being Catholic, he tells her if she marries me in a protestant church all her children will be bastard illegitimates and go to hell, I thumped him hard enough to break his holy jaw. Made Master 18th December 1909, sailed as 2nd and 3rd mate until I signed as 1st mate aboard the Letty. Skippered for Donald Curries trading primarily the Baltic. First Captain to take a ship through the minefields to Antwerp in 1918. It's in me blood the sea. There's salt in these scars. That's it.

guilt

as if the loss
were not enough

even when
the answer is yes

guilt in the bereaved

burrows wormlike

under the skin

into the conscience

laying eggs of doubt
which hatch questions

that gnaw and nag

did we, did we really,
do all that we could

The Chelmsford City feng-shui, burial and bully blues

1

this flat's too high
and dragons fly
where tigers ought to roam

let's get that old
feng-shui man
to relocate our home

2

bury me where the mountains rise
where the rivers come to a head

bury me beneath a forest green
but please make sure I'm dead

3

at school
Robert Thoroughgood
said I looked
like a taxi
with its doors open

HA HA HA
bleedin' wing nut;

last night
I shagged his missus

HA HA HA
bleedin' travelling salesman

Sonnet for Sharon

I'd like to take you rolling in the hay
Because I'm hornier than usual of late,
But you treat romantic gestures with dismay
And I've even heard you say the word 'castrate.'
Now, it's not as if I haven't taken steps,
To woo you now and then with gifts and treats,
And I know my boat race ain't like Johnny Depp's
And my nasal organ's like a parakeet's.
So just tell me what's a lonely boy to do?
I'm scrabbling around here in the dark,
 my ardour seems to make you want to spew
I might as well try doggin' in the park.
Oh Sharon, I am but a fool,
Darling I love you,
Though you treat me cruel.

cricket

breeze borne seeds of dandelion time
sway in a shimmering mirage
above the intense luminosity of rape

    a sublime cobalt sky stretches

                (reaches out)

    appearing to caress

    almost

the immaculate Victorian green beneath;

    and strangely

this feels like a moment of purest clarity

    just lying here
    on a manicured lawn

soaking up cherished bird song
and the willowy sounds of the lunatics
playing a game of soft slippered cricket

Cwm

...and sometimes at the end of a blind cwm where the black cloud is held low and shroudlike year round by a horseshoe of dark hills and the thunder echoes drummish against the rock and the grim lake swallows up the endless rain a man can watch three generations of the same family die in the same squat cottage the wind hammering at the doors of his sanity the fluke and the damp and the mould that took grandparents and parents and brothers alike leaving him with the weight of the world on his shoulders and the smell of the bog on his skin and god's biblical plagues of frog and fly and maggot and rotting white corpses pressing relentlessly upon his childlike humanity his yellow nails trimmed when they curl with sheers and his toothless jabber monotonous and long ago giving up on the journey to town or store or market now existing only on mutton or lamb cooked or otherwise and watching [*a lonely simian soul*] from the dank ffridd and cold barn the comings and goings of the shining girls with their tight clothes and golden hair swaying from side to side like the tails of beautiful ponies as they walk, watching with an acquisitive magpies eye and wondering aloud to himself if he could keep just one just for a little while just one just for a little while...

Campbell

Campbell had already blotted his copybook before the Battery deployed in Belfast, for shagging the Chaplain's daughter on a beach in Benbecula next to a bonfire made of stolen pews. The Troop Commander, Captain Goodman, known by the rank and file as Benny, a religious man and close friend of the Chaplain's, had vowed to keep an eye on Campbell and take revenge when the situation presented itself.

It didn't take long.

Benny made sure that wherever Campbell went he did too. So when F Troop were on an arms and explosives search of suspected Provo houses in the Ardoyne area of the city Benny instructed Campbell to carry and keep guard of his Sterling Sub Machine Gun while Benny searched and interrogated the Fenians.

Things didn't go well.

The Fenians simply told Benny to get fucked and no arms were found because the cunning I.R.A. had hidden their weapons where they thought soldiers probably wouldn't look.

Benny was disgruntled and a little sulky. He sat in silence in the Saracen and it wasn't until they were nearly back to base that he asked Campbell for his machine gun.

'Hand me my weapon Campbell,' he said.

It was a question that made Campbell fidget.

'Campbell,' Benny repeated.

'Sir,' Campbell replied.

'Where is my weapon Campbell?' Benny asked

Campbell's shrug and confused look took the Captain by surprise.

'For fuck's sake Campbell,' Benny shouted, 'my fucking weapon, I gave you my fucking weapon.'

'Not sure Sir.'

'Not fucking sure Campbell, what the fuck does that mean?'

Another shrug, 'Not sure Sir.'

'Jesus Christ Campbell you are a fucking idiot, a fucking idiot, I mean for Christ's sake man, what the fuck have you done with it?'

Another shrug.

The Captain shouted at the driver to turn the Saracen around and return to the houses they had visited earlier where, embarrassed and under duress, he had to knock on doors and ask the bemused home owners and suspected terrorists if, perhaps, he could please have his gun back.

Eventually the gun was found behind the settee of an alarmed old lady who pleaded her innocence with such vigour that she wet herself and the Captain felt obliged to offer her a lift to hospital in his armoured vehicle, a proposition so alarming to her that she fainted away and had to be left with a neighbour.

Further thoughts of revenge loomed large in Benny's consciousness and with this in mind he decided to call unannounced on Campbell when he was on guard duty in one of the camp's watch towers which overlooked the Battery's patch. If he could find him asleep, for example, there would be hell to pay.

So, one afternoon, knowing that Campbell was on a four hour duty, Benny gave him enough time to nod off and then slowly, and silently, began to make his way up the high ladders which led to the lookout sanger.

His plan had been to get to the metal hatchway that sealed the sanger and slowly raise it so as to peer in and catch Campbell asleep, or wanking, on duty. So he was a little surprised when he saw that the heavy metal hatch was already open and leaning against the sanger wall.

He was also surprised when he heard Campbell shout, 'Halt, who goes there?'

The captain stayed where he was. Half way up the third ladder.

'Halt, who goes there?' Campbell shouted again.

'Oh for fuck's sake Campbell,' Benny said, realising the game was up, 'don't be such a bloody fool. You know who it is.'

'Who goes there?' Campbell asked again.

'Stop being such a bloody idiot Campbell,' Benny shouted, 'it's me and I'm coming up. You'd better not have been sleeping in there or there'll be hell to pay.'

'Halt,' said Campbell, 'who goes there?'

Benny continued his climb and Campbell asked him one last time to halt and tell him who he was. Benny replied that he was a fucking idiot and that he knew who it was and, putting his hands onto the hatch to pull himself in, was taken by surprise when Campbell, on this occasion deciding that as a professional soldier valour was the better part of discretion, nudged the heavy hatch with his knee so that it slowly dropped onto the Captain's head, pole axing him, and sending him spiralling three sets of ladders down to the floor below.

When Campbell came out of the nick in Colchester, having done his time under The Black Watch, he told me that he thought it had all been worth it.

in car parks of America

case of cold Coors/Jack Daniel's Black

along the kerb
fire ants hurrying
industrious as the pick-ups
along the Camino Real

talking loudly of Hispanic girls

    of fighting

of the way the Welsh
are good with the dead and the dying

watching mushroom thunderclouds
    rise and flatten
beyond the Vegas Verde
    atomicpink
in a blousy Navajo sky
    shot through
with chromeshiny arrowheads

    later
at the Burrito Bus
tortas, tacos, mariscos,
the scary Chicano girl
with braided hair and rattlesnake skin
whispering obsidian-eyed bordertales
of El Paso cartels
of thirsty fruitjuice cartons
injected with sleeping drafts
of waking up naked
    drugged
robbed or worse
in Mexican emergency rooms

but it'll never happen to her
she's smart, got her spider sense,
always carries her blade

Mulatto Joe's & Pawn City
we buy guns/we sell knives

Santa Fe moonlight shining
jazzy on forgotten saxophones
sinister on racks of rifled gunmetal

and in the Pueblo a cruiser prowls

Gwenno

…see beautiful Gwenno's long black jackdaw hair and dark eyes deep as the dog lakes on Cnicht; see Gwenno's pale Snowdon lily skin shining white as death; see her full lips painted red as a dragon's tongue; see Gwenno in the square in Llanrwst tottering on heels higher than the mountain she lives on; see Gwenno's pot-bellied midriff exposed to sub-zero arctic conditions on the walk to parties in Penmachno; hear Gwenno's thunder thighs hissing under a skirt shorter than the name of her house on the hill; see Gwenno lobbing Lambrini bottles into the middle of fights in Ffestiniog; pressing her breasts into the backs of boys on barstools in bars in Blaenau; see Gwenno and her valley commandos launching night-time assaults on Conwy quay; see Gwenno shooting tequila slammers in bistros in Bangor; leaning out of limos in Llangefni; French kissing squaddies in the backs of taxis in Tregarth; listen to Gwenno laugh and shriek and howl and dance a crazy ballet druidic in her ruin and prophetic as a skunked dervish in clubs in Caernarfon; see wild Gwenno scaring all and sundry shitless in pubs in Pwllheli…

Cleopatra

a spectral tug perambulates,
bags pulsing like knuckled goitres,

she trawls bassooning Salvationists…

(There is an impact in sepia)

St. Michael's spinning udders
burst like rotten fruit in the street

a lifetime's collateral strewn in the gutter.

Meanwhile

a voyeur's hound laps condensation from
the Cooperative's window

a surgical taped post-card is revealed

Anubis is depicted with Osiris
they are guiding Queen Cleopatra
aboard the sun barge of Khnum

a good day to die

And he wonders how such a small death could end so many lives.

He loved him because he was his brother and he liked him because he was his friend and now in dark and sterile hotel rooms a bone-cold blue-granite pain brings him bright sunlit water memories of childhood; a small hand in a small hand in a small hand, reckless brothers-in-arms wading streams Zambezi-warm where Savannah air crackled grasshopper loud and the moorland pulsed in the pull of the sun, where climbing stones moss-greened slick to ford, they'd crouch Hawkeye still to await the Huron horde and paddle dragon-boats Viking quick across slate black Gwynant water or patrol mad-lancer,-like the Dervish, borders of their home.

He remembers a round boy in a square tank top. Tired legs on a metal steed. And how twice, selfless in his pain, his brother woke to see him sitting by the bed and how twice he raised his thumb and winked to say that all was well.

The sun rose cold-forged red that morning, the sky pristine blue and the grey crags boiled the cloud. His brother had waited for that day, for his dad to smooth his troubled brow, for his mum to tell him it was time to sleep, waited to hear the warriors' distant calling, 'it is a good day to die, when the sun is shining and the mist is in the sky.'

Now, wherever his wanderings take him, last thing at night, before sleep comes to take him back to Wales, he remembers how, at the very end, it was just him and his brother's newborn baby son and bereft young wife in that cottage on the hill and how he held her and how they wept and how he told her to look to her memories when the fog of grief clears, to think only of her brave boy smiling and happy in the heartland of his years.

And he wonders how such a small death could end so many lives.